Living & Loving

A. N. Triton

InterVarsity Press
Downers Grove, Illinois 60515

InterVarsity Press
is the book publishing
division of Inter-Varsity
Christian Fellowship.

ISBN 0-87784-548-4

Printed in the United
States of America

Contents

Preface

HE WOULD BE a fool who thought he could write the definitive book on the Christian view of sex. But this small collection of essays does try to deal with a number of the key issues of today. Some of the material I have taken over from an earlier book, *A Time to Embrace* . . ., including the chapter 'An Example of Victory' which was contributed by the Rev. J. G. K. Harman and the one entitled 'Prelude to Partnership' by John H. Paterson. Permission to include these articles is gratefully acknowledged. Chapters 1 and 9 are also revisions of material from this source. But most of the book is new.

In certain areas I have tried in some detail to apply basic biblical principles. But there will no doubt be other applications which each reader will want to make for himself. In the final resort each of us has to be fully persuaded in his own mind that he is pleasing God and that the way in which he is living in the body – the temple of the Holy Spirit – is in accordance with what God has told us in His written revelation. That revelation was given a long time ago, but its relevance to life today is not hard to find. We must rejoice in God's gift of our sexuality, and aim to live it out in gratitude to Him and in true love and consideration for others, knowing that His wisdom and His way are always best.

1 The Christian view of sex

Is SEX MADE for marriage or is marriage made for sex?

Taking the Bible as our guide, it is clear that sex is primarily for the lifelong friendship and partnership that we call marriage. Often, as a bonus, there is added a family. This biblical view of the matter stands in marked contrast to the ideas of those who regard sex as primarily for the propagation of the species or regard marriage as a purely optional way of dealing with our sex urges.

Man, the Bible tells us, is made to function in society. He can try to be a lone individual, and our background of nineteenth-century individualism may make this appear to be attractive. But we are intended to grow up in a family and in our turn to establish relationships with others of which the basic unit is the marriage relationship. If we are single, we are meant to find meaningful relationships of other kinds.

But sex is for marriage first of all, even though it may have a number of other excellent spin-offs, and marriage is primarily for friendship, though it also may have many other invaluable consequences. Children are a gift that God adds (and sometimes withholds) – a view of the matter that is too easily forgotten when the great subject of discussion is abortion.

Nevertheless the Christian church has not always spoken with one voice. The clear biblical teaching has too often been forgotten, through a desire to go along with the spirit of the times, or in an attempt to react against current abuses. If, for instance, the popular view of sex is purely biological, then one can understand some Christians being unconsciously brainwashed into the prevailing idea and others reacting into asceticism. And this has happened on a grand scale. Because they have treated sex as a purely animal function, many Christians have come to think that it is little more than a necessary evil with which they should have as little to do as possible. On that view celibacy is a virtue and necessary to leading a really spiritual life; sex is entirely for the procreation of children.

FRIENDSHIP

Needless to say, this totally misrepresents the biblical view. Eve was created because 'it is not good that the man should be alone', and she was to be a help meet for Adam. To be sure, God created man, male and female, and commanded them to replenish the earth and subdue it; but in the Bible the companionship and mutual help aspect of marriage always comes in the place of first importance. Even the 'one flesh' of marriage (Matthew 19 : 5) clearly refers to much more than physical union, because it is an alternative to dependence on parents. It must refer to a mutual dependence in all aspects of life.

Further, the Christian is free to marry only another Christian ('only in the Lord', 1 Corinthians 7 : 39), with the alternative of remaining unmarried. Those Christians who contemplate marrying a non-Christian show that they do not realize what sort of thing marriage is. They have forgotten the lifelong friendship of unequalled depth. They have been misled by modern thought into a superficial, biological or merely psychological view. The Old Testament also constantly stresses that these questions of personal religion always have priority in marriage. What is more, the main emphasis in New Testament teaching on marriage is on love, and Christ's relationship to His church is compared to the relationship of husband and wife (Ephesians 5 : 22–33), or rather, and more significantly, it is human marriage (which is the subject under discussion) which is compared to the relationship between the Lord and the church. This relationship is the most important element in marriage. Sex makes it possible and so gives the greatest of all kinds of human friendship. The ideal for the Christian is the love of Christ for His church and the church's responsive love.

But the fact that we are sexual beings also makes possible a variety of positive relationships short of marriage and greatly enriches human society. It adds enormously to the variety, depth, colour and enjoyment of life. It reduces, for instance, much of the loneliness, drabness and cold impersonality of the student world. It helps to make people gregarious rather than solitary.

How many students, who would otherwise be content to sit and overwork alone in a cold and poorly-furnished room, are, by the stirrings of sex, driven out into society and impelled to make their rooms a homely place of welcome? Other factors enter in as well, of course, and we cannot isolate sex from the rest of our nature. But there is no doubt that, consciously or unconsciously, sex has much to do with the good of society, friendship, culture and the spice of life.

THE FAMILY

The second purpose of sex according to the Bible is the bearing of children and the establishment of the family. The biological and psychological sides of marriage are seen by the Bible as God's good provision for the bringing up of children in a stable home. Man and wife are held together by sexual attraction and by the physical side of sex in a way that would otherwise be impossible. Deep and stable sexual love is a magnificent gift of God. One of its natural aims is a family and this is deeply ingrained in the psychology of both men and women. Sex is a very much wider thing than the physical relationships and we must fight the tendency to use the word only for its physical expression. This is not to suggest that the physical aspects of the marriage relationship are despised in the Bible. The apostles give brief practical commands on these things, too, and regard them as just as much part of God's good creation as the more 'spiritual' relationships. The Bible nowhere contrasts a good 'spirit' of man with an evil or inferior body. That is a Greek philosophical conception which is common in British thought today and has in the past sometimes dominated the church : but Christians must not give way to it.

The Christian should not therefore pretend to be a pale and disembodied 'saint', nor should he feel that purely Platonic love is higher than a fully-grown human love. It is not. God has given us bodies and minds to use. But man is not just an animal : he is not even primarily an animal. In a sense he is not an animal at all; he is a spiritual being, and that is something quite different. It is only useful to think of him as an animal for the purposes of those functions that he has fundamentally in common with them. Reproduction is one of these, but sex is not. For sex in man involves so much that never occurs in animals, and it is these specifically human aspects that are primary. Even the function of increasing the species must not be seen in man as if it was something merely biological. 'Children are an heritage of the Lord' and must be seen primarily as a human and a spiritual responsibility and blessing. The family is a far greater thing than merely perpetuating the race.

Even from the purely biological point of view the aim of sex is not romantic or erotic satisfaction, but the bringing up of a family in a stable and healthy home. To idolize those physical aspects of sex, which, even biologically speaking, are only a means to an end, is to court disaster on the biological and psychological level, as well as on the spiritual level. The modern cult of sex turns out in fact to be not a cult of sex at all, but a worship of only one aspect of sex. Sex is a far bigger thing than this, and if we separate it on the one hand from its fully human context (friendship) and on the other from its biological goal (family), we are left with an idol that cannot repay our worship even in terms of human satisfaction. To propose sexual intercourse outside the relationship of entire commitment to live in love and care for one another, which is possible only in marriage, is a gross insult. It implies that the partner is wanted simply for our own satisfaction. It differs from prostitution only in degree, and in the fact that it is cheaper.

THE CHRISTIAN ESTIMATE OF MARRIAGE

Both sex and marriage were ordained before the Fall, and although the Fall has added a third reason for marriage, that is to direct our instincts into the best paths and, in a sinful world, to make their proper use easier (1 Corinthians 7 : 1–3), this has not altered in any way the primary purposes of sex. It is, in the writer's view, a great pity that, in the Prayer Book marriage service, the primary reason for marriage has been put third and this has therefore tended to obscure in people's minds the essentially positive biblical view of marriage as one of God's great and good gifts given for our mutual fellowship and for the increase of mankind in the best possible way. Sex was originally one of the aspects of the creation that was 'very good', and still today in a fallen world we are taught by the apostle Paul to say that 'everything created by God is good' (1 Timothy 4 : 4), and to believe that this includes sex and marriage, which latter is one of the subjects dealt with specifically by the apostle in this passage.

IS SEX SINFUL?

The Christian, then, should not be ashamed of sex. He may perhaps be a little frightened of its power, but like every other great gift he must accept it thankfully and with wonder at the wisdom and love of God. If we stop to think about it at all, we should be driven to astonished and grateful worship that God has devised such a means of enriching our society and ensuring for each new generation both loving care and the passing on of our cultural heritage. And all this in a way that even our sinful nature cannot altogether steal from us. Those who least acknowledge God may enjoy many of its benefits, and some of those who are most selfish and depraved can be tamed and restored to a useful place in society by the imperious demands of a pure and stable sexual love.

This does not appear to solve our problems, however, and the ordinary student may be impatient about such generalities. Our situation is an intensely practical one. We find ourselves powerfully attracted by members of the opposite sex; what is more, that attraction is at least in part a physical attraction. We are neither married nor can many of us have any reasonable prospect of early marriage. What are we to do with these instincts and mutual attractions? Are they sinful and to be suppressed? Do they border on the 'looking lustfully' of Matthew 5:28? If not, how can we regard them and turn them to good?

If what has been said so far is true, then the fact that we find the opposite sex attractive is not sinful. In fact it is good and right. But we are fallen, and the effect of our sinfulness is that we tend to misuse sex and are in danger of getting the whole thing so unbalanced that we spoil it. Thus we are tempted to be selfish and merely pleasure-seeking on the one hand, and on the other, to find that the attractiveness of the opposite sex, which is perfectly right in itself, easily becomes an occasion of evil thoughts and wrong desires. 'To the pure all things are pure', says the apostle (Titus 1 : 15). If we were not the sinners we are, we could constantly be thanking God for beautiful or handsome bodies and attractive personalities without fear of such thoughts turning over into something not altogether pure.

Our Lord's words in Matthew 5 : 27–30 refer primarily, of course, to married persons, and if people never allowed themselves to think that their beloved was extremely desirable they would never be likely to get married. But our Lord's warning applies also to the unmarried. Such thinking easily goes bad on you. The characteristic result of the Fall is to make an idol of something good, and we all know how easily in this sphere our thoughts can become sensual, selfish and impure, especially when there is no real love involved. In fact sensuality is best defined as exalting the physical into an improper place. Where there is no real love the merely physical attraction has to be kept very severely in its place, and when there is true love it ceases to be the main thing and becomes subordinate. If we allow the physical to dominate our thinking or our relationship, we have got things in a quite false perspective. The very elementary biblical emphasis on love as the first duty is the only true corrective. But love in the New Testament is not merely an emotion. It is a practical concern for the other's good. This is something infinitely better which can direct all else into its rightful place. We must often ask ourselves whether our attraction for someone is really love or just selfish, whether it is true friendship or merely exciting.

THE HIGHEST VIEW OF SEX

The Christian, therefore, has to fight a constant battle against the popular ideas of sex. It is not that he holds a low view of sex as something evil. On the contrary, it is because he holds such a high view of it that he cannot allow it to be reduced to a merely physiological or psychological phenomenon, or regard it merely as a means of pleasure. He may often appear to the outside world to be much too restrained and stiff. But a similar situation obtains, for instance, about money. The Christian appears to be stupidly economical and even miserly because he has a high view of money as a gift to be used for the best. He believes that it should not be wasted or spent merely selfishly. As the *nouveau riche* is notoriously and ridiculously inclined to be spendthrift, so also those who are young and for whom sex is a relatively new wealth are tempted more than others to be undisciplined. Unfortunately the attack in the matter of sex is more subtle and plausible than in the matter of money. Under the guise of being 'natural' we are often presented with an entirely unbalanced and wrong set of ideals. Sex is natural, of course, but its exploitation can often be dressed up as something so entirely 'right' and even 'holy' that it is easy to lose our balance. We may compare the person who is easily drawn into drunkenness in order to 'be a man' or to enjoy himself. In fact, nothing makes a person less of 'a man' than drunkenness or an undisciplined use of sex. Nothing makes a girl less of a woman than deliberate display of mere sensual attractiveness. That is the art used to provoke a merely sensual response by those who are incapable

17

of love. It is easy to fall into the trap of trying to 'impress' or 'attract' the opposite sex by emphasizing our sexuality and so cheapening all our relationships. It is terribly immature, and a dangerous start. Here the Women's Liberation movement have a good point when they say that women must not be primarily sex symbols. That is to debase womanhood. And parallel things should be said about men.

We all know that in marriage the physical side will have to retire to take a secondary place in relation to the constant mutual love and care of one another which are the basis of everyday living. It is probably a failure to see this that has more than anything else contributed to the instability of marriage. The biological side is a good servant but an intolerable master, and it must be a servant from the beginning; no position is more honourable. If we allow it to dominate, and those who practise pre-marital intercourse do just that, it is the devil let loose.[1] It is the worst possible preparation for marriage, where it must always be secondary, and it is desperately hard to recover one's balance and to get true love and friendship put first.

FLIRTATION

This explains in part why Christians cannot allow the flirtation and experimentation that are so acceptable in some circles. These represent a complete misunderstanding of what man is and of what is the place of his God-given instincts. To experiment with them in a wrong use not only gives no idea of their right use, but almost always distorts the whole picture. It injures our

[1] See also pp. 29–40.

relationship to God, warps our attitude to sex and corrodes our capacity truly to love. Even a little flirtation does real harm. The men and women who are chaste in deed and thought are not to be pitied as immature and ignorant; they are to be envied as healthy and strong, with their latent powers still unspoiled.

If it is asked how we can know we are right for each other unless we do experiment a bit, the answer would seem to be that, while true friendship leads to our doing more and more together, and thus getting to know one another and our reactions better, flirtation is a non-loving experimentation – a playing around with other people to see what happens or to get a kick out of it for ourselves. It cannot tell you what you want to know. There is sheer, old-fashioned selfishness in this. To behave in this way, not only in sleeping together but in arousing sex in an irresponsible way, is to exploit someone else for our own satisfaction. It can cause tremendous havoc. As the proverb has it, 'Like a madman who throws firebrands, arrows, and death, is the man who deceives his neighbour and says, "I am only joking!"' (Proverbs 26 : 18, 19). The irresponsible hit-and-miss approach, where superficial affection is easily given and easily transferred, results in someone being seriously hurt before long.

Yet those people who talk the most about unselfish and spontaneous love are sometimes most guilty of it. To excuse their selfish lack of discipline they call every passing fancy 'love' and then say that they made a simple 'mistake', which surely is not blameworthy. If you play around with a loaded revolver in a crowd it is your fault when someone is shot.

It is very doubtful whether anyone has ever suffered

psychological injury by a sound discipline when it is coupled with a positive and biblical ideal of sex. This does not rule out strong friendships where there is real love, but one cannot experiment with love any more than one can experiment with the physical aspects of sex, or it ceases to be the genuine thing immediately and becomes an end in itself. There is a world of difference between conscious and deliberate suppression and what is psychologically termed repression. The latter involves an attempt to forget and to escape from reality. The former faces the facts and seeks to bring our nature under control. Repression is dangerous, but it is altogether healthy and right to be self-controlled.

To some people, however, there remains a lurking suspicion that the Christian standards are not really 'natural'. At times they seem to go so much against the grain. We are inclined to be very sympathetic with the characters in fiction, or in real life, who abandon restraint or morality when they find it overwhelmingly 'natural' to do so. Of course, the Christian standards do not pander to our fallen and selfish nature. But it is clear that the Bible sees God's restraints and commands in this matter as directing us into the *truly* natural path – that is to say, into the path in which our whole nature can work as it was created by God to work. This will always be essentially the best, even if it does not correspond with our 'get-rich-quick' mentality. The good is often the enemy of the best, and if we are to avoid certain things, which are very attractive and seem even to be good in themselves, it is because God has something much better for us. Therefore He forbids some things and commands others. Christian sexual morality is not a way of depriving us of pleasure but a way of giving us some of the greatest human gifts there are – stable and trustful marriage relationships, and healthy and stimulating relationships between the sexes outside marriage. We can enjoy the latter with enthusiasm just because we know (or ought to be able to assume) that there are limits which the other will not cross. So we can enjoy friendship with a girl or boy most freely when we know that immorality is simply not on. He or she is just not going to play that game and therefore both of us are going to control petting and stop well before it becomes a natural prelude to sleeping together. The negative rule increases our freedom and our enjoyment.

Far from being essentially negative, Christian morality is always positive in its *aim*. For this reason we are justified in trying to persuade non-Christians to follow Christian standards. They are ultimately the best and most conducive to happiness, and we should not hesitate to show them that this is so. It is like the exacting rules for physical training – negative often in form (don't drink, don't eat certain kinds of food, don't stay up late, *etc.*), but positively concerned with making us really fit. So Paul compares the Christian life to an athletic contest and stresses the need for continuous discipline if we are to win the prize (1 Corinthians 9 : 24–27). Therefore we should be firm with ourselves and with others. To start trying to live as if there were no fixed principles is to be at best a fool and, if we know what we are doing, a culpable danger to others and a rebel against God.

MASTURBATION

At this point a very brief word about masturbation may be in place. By this we mean the rather common practice of solitary, physical sexual gratification. It is nowhere explicitly condemned in the Bible and is not, therefore, the same kind of issue as fornication. But as in many other questions of this kind, the Bible gives us some general principles that we must try to apply, and in the absence of any statement dealing with this matter directly we have to work out our attitude from these principles. Impure fantasy and lustful thoughts and imaginations, for instance, which are often, but not always associated with it, are clearly included in the repeated condemnation of 'impurity'. Ephesians 5:3, 4, for example, puts it like this: 'But immorality (*i.e.* fornication) and all impurity and covetousness must not even be named among you, as is fitting among saints. Let there be no filthiness . . .' Whenever such things as these are associated with an action, then, according to the Bible, such behaviour is wrong. If they are no part of it, and if we have a clear conscience before God on the matter, then the decision whether or not to indulge in this practice must be made on other grounds.

For example, Paul in Romans 14, when discussing practical decisions on which Christians are not unanimous, lays down the general rule, 'whatever does not proceed from faith is sin' (verse 23). If, then, we have any doubt at all in any matter, we must seek God's grace to avoid behaviour which, though it may not be wrong in itself, is not something that we personally find that we can do before God with confidence.

But even if we were to feel that we could accept masturbation as being in our case a right and natural means of release from tensions and pressures built up by our way of life, we still cannot regard it as the ideal solution. Sex is truly itself only when it is expressed in a situation of mutuality – of give and take. Masturbation focuses in myself and has no compensating benefits. There is no release from loneliness and no increase in self-awareness. Indeed in these respects it may make things worse. To argue for it on the grounds that it is simply pleasurable, for instance, is therefore quite inadequate. The fact that we find pleasure or a kind of release in something so self-centred, and tending to increasing self-centredness, indicates that much further back something is not right.

The answer, then, is not to break our heart over the symptoms of the disorder, but to bring to God the problems it lays bare. It shows us that we are not adjusted in this area of our lives. It exposes our personal immaturity and probably our spiritual immaturity as well. In this sense it is like losing one's temper, or having a row with one's fiancée, which may clear the air and in some sense be a good thing considering the situation that has built up. But the situation it deals with is one to be regretted and we try to ensure that it is not repeated, though that may take time to work out. So with masturbation. Perhaps we needlessly stimulated the tension from which we now seek release. Perhaps for a long time our thoughts have been allowed to run on in wrong channels. Perhaps it expresses a general lack of self-control so that we tend, in many areas, to be easily turned aside from what is good by what is immediately attractive. Even when it is considered in its most favourable light it is therefore likely to be a humiliating experience as these things are exposed.

It is also, of course, a terribly mean sort of experience compared with the experience of sex within marriage. As we have stressed, physical sex really makes sense only in the setting of marriage. Masturbation is extraordinarily unsatisfactory and, if it becomes a habit, can distort our attitude to sex within marriage in the same sort of way that constant flirtation distorts our attitude to love within marriage. If people reply that, as far as they are concerned, masturbation has nothing to do with marriage or love, but is nevertheless of some value in their situation, then one can only say that they will have to watch these dangers. It could easily demean their attitude to the physical intimacies of marriage and become a substitute for, and a hindrance to, going out and making friends with members of the other sex as we are intended to do.

In the end, therefore, we find very few Christians who are able to argue for it as something which is right and good, and not in some sense to be regretted before God. Yet the trouble is not in the thing itself, but rather in what it represents, or in the frankly evil things that may go with it or give rise to it. 'Let every one be fully convinced in his own mind', says Paul (Romans 14 : 5); and let him also be sure that he is being really honest about it.

SUBLIMATION

Timothy, who may or may not have been married, was told to regard the younger women as 'sisters' (1 Timothy

24

5 : 2) and this sets a high standard of consideration, restraint and respect for their personality and privacy, as well as a certain dignity of relationship which is all too often lost with regard to other people's sisters or brothers. It is very easy to become either undignified and silly, or else unduly personal and inquisitive. True friendship is not established by either.

We want to use the fact that we are made sexual beings in the best ways. While we are unattached we can let it enrich all our social life. We can learn to enjoy the kind of friendship and partnership which only mixed society provides. But we must not get it out of proportion or allow it to rob us of the often deeper and more open friendships with people of our own sex. These have been traditionally one of the best features of student life and we should not throw them away. There is often a rare beauty of character and fulfilment seen in the face of a mother who has lovingly, unselfishly and with immense patience and faith brought up a family, been a true partner to her husband and taken the strains of the home. But there is an equally great beauty in the face of many single women whose natural sexual urges have been sublimated into other forms of loving service, and constructive, unselfish friendships and different roles in society. Sublimation may not be a very popular idea today, but we ought to acknowledge that in some degree it is necessary for all of us, and there is this marvellous capacity of men and women, when their gifts and faculties do not find their most natural outlets, not just to repress and allow them to atrophy, but to turn them to good for others and for themselves in different ways. Self-pity is no solution at all and turns everything it touches sour. If our love has been unreturned, or if we think of ourselves as 'on the shelf', we can look for means of sublimating our sexuality in positively useful and rewarding ways. Some of the unhappiest people in the world are married. The happiest, most fulfilled and satisfied include not a few who are single and have sublimated their energies constructively.

SOME PRACTICAL RULES

At the risk of seeming over-dogmatic, it is probably worth while to suggest the following practical rules which might be applied to ourselves.

1. We shall welcome opportunities of constructive relationship and working together with the opposite sex, knowing that outside marriage, as well as within it, each has different gifts and a different outlook to bring, and that we can learn from, and be influenced for good by, the other. We should take the opportunities of learning to appreciate their solid qualities.

2. We shall learn to appreciate one another for the qualities that really matter and try to keep mere physical attraction from looming too large in our thinking. 'Charm is deceitful, and beauty is vain, but a woman who fears the Lord is to be praised' (Proverbs 31 : 30). We shall dress and behave so as not to make mere physical attraction obtrude in the minds of others. Those who dress to kill are commonly said to cook in the same manner! There is sometimes a difficult distinction between being 'well got up' and being deliberately attractive sexually. The distinction is as much in

our minds and attitudes as in the outward form of dress and appearance, though it affects both.

3. Because we value real friendship we shall set our face against superficially exciting friendships and flirtations. We should be beyond the teen-age mentality that needs to be constantly paired off or even to be constantly on the lookout for a possible partner. We cannot prevent these things coming into our thoughts but we can keep them under control, and as Christians, who have learnt to trust the Lord, we can commit the matter to Him and be patient.

4. We shall never deliberately arouse sexual feelings and desires unless we are deeply in earnest and it is done in a context of true love. Sex is too fine a gift to be so debased. Other people's personalities are too precious to play with. Not many girls seem to realize how explosively stimulating the exposure of the feminine form can be to men. Not many men seem to realize how explosive a little careless fondling can be to a girl.

5. We shall seek always to desire God's will for us personally, knowing that what He decides is best, however difficult. In particular, we shall recognize that as students we may have to postpone thoughts of marriage because of our studies or our lack of money, or because for the next few years we believe we are called to some form of Christian service in which marriage is inappropriate. We do well to try to settle this in our minds and to be content before God to leave this on one side for the next few years, if this is His will. We must also think and pray over the whole question of marriage and

27

face the fact that it may not be God's plan for us. We must not regard it as a right.

6. We shall treat sex and all the questions associated with it with respect and dignity. Jokes about it are mostly out of place. A joke always deflates its subject. We can laugh at the erratic behaviour of a courting couple, but we cannot laugh at either marital faithfulness or marital unfaithfulness without making them trivial. We must seek always to treat members of the opposite sex with honour, respect and a certain necessary reserve or restraint.

7. Above all, we shall guard our thought-life and keep the highest Christian ideals before us. We must not, for instance, descend to a view of marriage which is less than a rich human friendship between Christian partners. We must avoid phantasy. We must sift what we read. We must make the whole question a matter of thankful prayer. Here scriptural commands guide us (*e.g.* Colossians 3 : 1, 2; Ephesians 5 : 4; Philippians 4 : 8). When tempted to evil thoughts we should set our minds on the 'divine opposite', including a thankful remembrance of the right purpose of sex, the biblical view of marriage and the great ideals set before us in the Bible in this respect.

2 Why shouldn't we?

IT IS COMMONLY believed today that, if a boy and girl love one another, then there is no real objection to their sleeping together. 'All you need is love' is, amongst other things, regarded as a justification for sexual freedom. Un-married sex, it is argued, could be a genuine expression of love and respect. It might seal a relationship that is valid and honourable. To those involved there is often something really marvellous about it. They may feel they want to thank God for such a superb way of expressing their love. If God made them with these aspects of their nature, and built into such a friendship the further possibilities that sleeping together could give, why should their love not be fulfilled in this way?

It may be best to start with the extreme example. An engaged couple are really in love. They seriously intend to marry. Financial and professional factors, however, make this very difficult just now. She is trying to finish her course in medicine. He wants to finish his Ph.D. and get a regular job before they settle down. They see each other almost entirely at week-ends. They feel that the pain of constant parting and the misery of a long wait for marriage would be so naturally alleviated and their love so admirably expressed and probably cemented by 'going the whole way' physically. 'Why shouldn't we?' they ask.

It is as well to look first at some of the serious arguments on the side of 'freedom'. First of all there is the question of what in any case constitutes a marriage? Is it really just a ceremony and some sentences pronounced over them in church? Surely what matters is their determination to live together for a lifetime and to share everything in a marriage partnership? Why wait for the ceremony before physical union? Is the ceremony any more fundamental than buying a flat? Yet no-one objects in principle to marriage without a home.

Secondly, delay could wreck the relationship. Desire is strong and restraint sets up strains and stresses. They are both at times somewhat irritable. There is an artificiality about drawing the line in the degree of petting that they feel is proper for an engaged couple. There is from time to time the fear that unless they begin to sleep together they could lose one another. Will someone in his lab. play upon his pent-up sexual emotion and encourage him to find some satisfaction in a relationship at work? There seems to be rather a lot of attractive girls in the department. And what about her? Will the strain do her psychological harm? Could it even damage their relationship when it comes to marriage? Isn't it cruel and wrong to demand such restraints from

perience, but that is a childish way of looking at it. One is not so surprised when younger teen-agers experiment with sex, because they are often incapable of viewing life as a whole, and in a permissive society all they can see is an apparently pleasant experience. But if people are old enough to think in terms of lifelong friendships, then they should be capable of thinking long-term and refusing immediate satisfaction for the sake of future and greater good. If they are capable of saving money for the home, they should be capable of saving sexual experience in the same way.

It is hard to over-emphasize how important this is. In the Christian ideal stable marriage is the great thing. Sex is made for marriage, not vice versa. God made us like this so that even selfish people could enjoy a lifelong partnership with all its benefits. This has tremendous potentiality for good for the partners, for the children and for society. It is true that a polygamous society can be sociologically stable – at the expense of the status of women and the partnership between man and wife. It is true that a society with frequently changing mates (or freely changeable) could conceivably be elaborated into a stable community : but it would be at the expense of the children and to the destruction of the rich friendships that grow out of the years of partnership, through the vicissitudes of child-rearing, illness, *etc*. Nothing could be a more shattering blow to the welfare of the retired generation, which is now so large a part of our Western society. The life of so many of these is made satisfying and useful only by the mature partnership of their husband or wife and the affection of, or at least contact with, the children they have themselves brought up since birth. One could go on thinking of possible

35

alternatives and the price they would exact of our society. But the Christian conviction is that God's plan is unequivocally best because He, our living Creator, made it. He knows exactly how society works best and even if we cannot see it He would not have commanded it without excellent reason. The Law of God is always good. It is always the best for mankind in the long run and it should be for us acceptable, even if it seems to place us in a tough spot (see Romans 12 : 1, 2).

This in fact is part of the problem. If our society makes it hard for a couple to marry, they can complain that the fault is not in God's ideal, which they recognize, but in the impossible situation in which they are placed. Perhaps, like some students today, they are so thrown together and live and work together from morning to late at night in their bed-sitters that they feel the strain is well-nigh impossible. How could such a life be other than highly stimulating sexually? Yet marriage seems often out of the question.

Now everyone must agree that there are tough cases. But that is no excuse for self-pity. If we are under strain we can equally regard it as a privilege to be allowed to fight in a tough spot and to develop some moral fibre as a result. In a day when discipline is at a discount this may not be a popular idea. But there is no doubt that some of those who have really faced and overcome difficulties have been the people who in the long run have given most to society and been of greatest use to others. The homes that are founded on self-restraint are the better for it and better able to contribute to others. If they think that there is a danger of delay wrecking the relationship, there is also an equal danger of licence wrecking it, or of establishing it on a

36

basis of selfish impulse that is a very poor foundation for the future. In the home there is going to be a tremendous need for discipline and unselfishness. There will be need for restraint and self-control on just this same level of sexual desire. Selfishness in sexual intercourse has wrecked many marriages. There will be a need for positive thoughtfulness for one another and restraint for the sake of each other and the children. No-one should think of the marriage service as a licence for greed. It is a door into a freer expression of *love*, but love, if genuine, is essentially unselfish and therefore restrains us.

This is one of the problems admirably discussed by C. S. Lewis in *The Four Loves*.[1] Sexual desire is different from true love. It is somewhat selfish. If it is not in a context of genuine unselfish love for a person it is the devil let loose. The fact is that, if we really love our partner, we will not wish to encourage or to co-operate with him or her in what is not the best, or in something that can so easily be a degradation of our relationship. So many engagements and lesser friendships, far from being cemented by sexual intercourse, have at that very point begun to degenerate and to disintegrate.

There are also plenty of other human reasons for restraint. It is easily forgotten how often intercourse arouses in a woman, and even in many men, a deep and imperious desire for children. Outside marriage, therefore, it can make matters far worse. The student psychologists point out fairly frequent cases where unmarried pregnant girls show all the signs of having deliberately relaxed their contraceptive precautions ('just that once, Doctor'), probably because of an only

[1] London, Fontana, 1963.

half-conscious but passionate desire for a baby. Once a couple have embarked on intercourse, therefore, the strain of not being married and still so far from any hope of a family can become a cruel injury. If, before, the strains were severe, they can easily now become much worse. Intercourse opens out also all kinds of lesser personal intimacies. It is an entirely artificial position to be meeting only occasionally for such profound expression of love and to be at the same time cut off from normal married life. This is also, of course, an argument against getting married when you cannot live together in a fairly normal way; but at least when you are married it is easier to share life when you do see each other and to be entirely relaxed and free in one another's presence and in the presence of others. If premature intercourse forces us into a clandestine relationship, we are sadly spoiling some wonderful and enriching aspects of what marriage is meant to be and placing ourselves under some very destructive strains and stresses.

After all, marriage is not primarily just being able to sleep together. It is primarily a full-orbed fellowship and partnership in which the physical has to take its important but not dominant position. By pressing ahead on the physical aspect we unbalance the whole experience. It should move forward on all levels at once. If we are not yet ready to 'go the whole way' in public commitment to one another for life, and not yet ready to live together on the broadest human basis, we are not yet ready to 'go the whole way' in a narrowly physical expression of our love. If we do, we give the reins to the purely physical side of marriage, and that is a travesty of the great thing it is meant to be. Love is not just

38

expressed physically and, as we all know, it is extremely easy to deceive ourselves and others about this and to mistake physical attraction and the selfish seeking of physical satisfaction for genuine love. It is right that we should be made to prove the genuineness of our love by our willingness to marry before we grasp what is so easily grasped selfishly, and discarded selfishly when the excitement and novelty have begun to wear off. There seems to be at least some direct connection between the current emphasis on the purely physical side and the instability of so many marriages today. Physical desire is not a stable or constant thing. It is sure to fluctuate and ultimately to fade. If this is given the lead role our whole relationship is bound to be unstable. From the start it must be our servant and not our master. It is no accident that many marriages become unstable when the parents reach their forties and the purely physical attractions begin to wane.

All this is well illustrated by 1 Corinthians 6, where Paul discusses extra-marital sexual experiences. He makes the at first sight surprising comment that it is a 'sin against the body'. Quite apart from its being a sin before God, it is an affront and injury to the body. This seems not only to mean that it is a misuse in theory and in principle, but that it is likely to do damage, and the context makes plain that he has personality damage rather than narrowly physical damage in mind. That is not to say that there are measurable injuries which we can chalk up as the inevitable consequences of every act of fornication. But it is not only an insult to God; it is also an insult to our created nature and that of our partner, and such insults are very rarely unrequited.

Sin does find us out in this life as well as in the next

39

and this is peculiarly true in this area where, as the passage says, our body and personality are included in a way that is not true to the same degree of any other kind of sin. The Christian standards therefore are not only for Christians. We cannot, for instance, feel that, so long as we take a temporary holiday from active Christianity, we can then go and live as we like. We can never escape from the Creator's order of nature. Whether we are Christians or not, fornication is a sin against the body and we shall pay a sad price for it. But God does not take any pleasure in that. Therefore He tells us how to live in His world. And to the Christian especially, the love of God and gratefulness for His good and health-giving commands are an over-riding reason for living as He wants. Indeed sexual sin is somehow a peculiarly mean and childish grasping at immediate pleasure without respect for what is really good. Its meanness is seen, however, only when you stop to think what great and marvellous gifts God has given us in marriage – the richest of all earthly blessings when it is enjoyed as God intends us to enjoy it. Go and talk frankly to a happily married couple and the whole thing will be seen in a more balanced perspective.

3 What about petting?

THE KEY QUESTION is not whether we have sex before marriage, but in what ways and in what degree we express our sexuality before marriage. The totally a-sexual person is a figure of fiction and we must come to terms with the fact that God gave us our sexuality. But if so, what does He expect us to do about it? Is it to be entirely dormant until marriage? Fairly obviously the answer is 'No'. We cannot pretend that we do not notice the beautiful girl or the attractive boy, or that we fail to find a different kind of pleasure in friendships with the opposite sex from friendships with our own sex. And that is one of the things that greatly enriches life and for which we have every reason to be thankful.

The problem is really this: What kind of expression of our sexuality is appropriate to our friendships? There is a stage when just catching his or her eye and getting a smile is reward enough to give us a blissful week-end. But there are also stages when we desperately want close physical contact and we know we must keep control of ourselves or we shall do and say things that will do damage. It is a long spectrum of increasing desire as we get to know and like each other better. It escalates naturally to a point where there is no real satisfaction short of marriage. This is assuming, of course, that it does so progress. We know all too well that many such friendships stop half way or peter out. Even just at the point of engagement they may fail, and that is something we obviously have to keep in mind. We must not do what we shall later regret.

What, then, is a Christian assessment of petting? We wish to propose three principles. First, and fairly obviously, there are different modes of expressing one's affection which are *appropriate* to each stage of such a relationship. We want to express ourselves fittingly. Too much reserve may choke natural and entirely wholesome progress. Too much physical freedom can either mean that the physical aspect of our relationship takes the control and gets out of balance, or it can lead to a revulsion of feeling because we sense that we are being guided by mere biological drives and not by friendship or real love. We have a tendency to let our actions go ahead of our hearts and our minds. The whole process tends to accelerate in a perfectly understandable way. At first holding hands is a great privilege. Then it begins to seem a bit tame. Somewhat timidly perhaps at first it leads to caressing and kissing. Kissing gets hotter and caressing more demanding. Then we realize that we have got to call a halt. Yet the old stimuli do not now produce quite the same result. The law of diminishing returns comes into operation and we have to decide whether we are going to keep up the pace or let this side of our relationship play a lesser part.

Second, a great deal depends on what kind of a relationship it is. Is it friendship or a flirtation, for instance? In the anonymity of student life we want to belong. The obvious way to belong is to pair off. This can be an entirely selfish affair. We want a partner because it is socially convenient for us both, it is a boost to our egos and in any case it is nice to be in the fashion. None of these reasons are wrong in themselves, but they do not constitute a friendship of even the mildest kind. If that is the kind of relationship it is, then we ought to recognize that physical demonstration of affection is pure hypocrisy. There is no real affection in it and the man or woman who wants to kiss just because it is the fashion is at best exceedingly cheap. Of course, such a relationship of convenience may grow into real love, but it will not do that because of petting. Indeed petting is likely to turn it into a mere flirtation where we are so preoccupied with the physical stimuli that we have not enough initiative left to develop it as a worth-while friendship.

Few things are so devastating to deep and lasting friendship as allowing ourselves to be led on by increasing petting. One has met couples whose very promising and worth-while relationships have been quite ruined by allowing them to be dominated by it. After a while their anticipation of meeting was chiefly physical. If they could not pet they did not know what to do or to talk about. They were driven therefore to meet less and less in worth-while activities together, or in company with others, and more and more in contexts where they had scope for petting and very little else. After a while this comes to a crisis. Either they have got to get married – and they have no adequate basis for it – or they have to part company. They can hardly go back to square one and try to develop a normal friendship and courtship. The basic reason is that the physical relationship got out of control and totally out of balance. The non-Christians who allow this situation to push them into sleeping together so often find that they are heartily sick of the relationship before long. Generally the man gets tired first, and the girl realizes too late that he is not willing to offer her the security she needs, and could find only in marriage. She then breaks it up by looking for another man who will give her what she craves. This happens constantly in student life, and each blames the other. According to the statistics a high proportion of students who are sexually 'experienced' also change their partners before long. The fact is that there is too little in the relationship for it to last or for it to maintain the intimacies involved in sleeping together.

Third, we have to examine our motives and our ambitions. What do we really value in life and what do we want to be and to do? Are we merely determined to get our man or our girl while there is a good choice? Do we think of marriage rather as the materialist thinks of a job – a means of making life more pleasant and easier and more satisfying? If so, then of course the thing is to find the nicest partners in sight and try to hook them. That is where the major excuse for excessive petting comes : you have to do it or allow it (admittedly a bit prematurely) because, it is said, that is the only way to catch and keep a good partner. But that is a lie.

A worth-while partner will be found and kept through the sort of affection that will stand complete deprivation of physical contact. If the relationship depends on petting you can hardly let one another out of sight because several months of separation (quite common in married life) could leave you with no real ties. Such an approach to marriage has its reward – a 'nice' partner, maybe – but usually absolutely nothing more.

The Christian's motives and his trust are frankly different from those of most other people. He knows that God has a plan for each stage of his (or her) life. If he is going to enjoy being paired off, it is because he believes it is a God-given friendship which is intended to enrich both and to make both better able to serve others. The selfish elements have got to be kept in their place. It is no good pretending that they are not there, but they have got to be made to serve God's purposes and not just our own impulses. The Christian does not want to get deeply involved, therefore, until he is sure that the friendship is meant to be lasting. Far from wanting to hook the partner, he or she is concerned to discover what is God's plan and then to follow this out.

For most of us God's plan is ultimately marriage but, as a rule, while we are students, it is His future plan. We do not need to fret, to seek 'experience', or to fight for a partner. We are trying to serve God in the path He sees is best. That could mean going it alone for a long stretch. If we are paired off it certainly means trying to make the friendship as constructive as possible and that involves keeping the physical side in the background. (James 4 : 1–3 applies, with little adaptation.) Although marriage is not specifically mentioned, our

45

Lord's words in Matthew 6 : 33 cover the whole of life in its human aspects : 'Seek first his kingdom and his righteousness, and all these things shall be yours as well.' In the context He agrees that there are fatuous human rewards for grasping often lesser aims ('They have their reward'); but the Christian is taught to see through such relative trivialities.

These are three principles which we each can apply to our own situation. Finally we add a few purely practical observations. The man is liable to take any liberties that the girl allows and then say it is her fault. Therefore it is often up to the girl to say 'No' and the man will respect her the more if she does. Often he is just testing the situation out rather carelessly and has never thought to a conclusion what is, and what is not, right. He expects her to drive with one foot on the brake while his is on the accelerator. This is frankly mean of him and shows lack of real thoughtfulness. Just because her reactions are often more emotional and less rational than his, he needs to take the responsibility and *think* it out. Otherwise he is really taking advantage of her and abdicating his proper masculine role.

It is one of the gifts of God that women are more slowly aroused physically than men but that, when they are aroused, they find it much harder just to forget it. Therefore a man has got to be very careful not to arouse passions needlessly. The Song of Solomon, whatever its primary purpose, is a love song which has done an enormous amount to create an ideal of pure sexual love which is certainly full-blooded and not lacking in physical elements. But it is the Song of Solomon, with all its positive attitude to sex, that includes the warning : 'I adjure you, O daughters of Jerusalem, that you stir not up nor awaken love until it please'; and one reason, given a few verses later, is 'Many waters cannot quench love, neither can floods drown it' (Song 8 : 4, 7). That is another reason why flirtation is wicked. It can permanently sour another life by arousing almost unquenchable passions.

Biologically it is quite clear that petting is part of the natural prelude to sleeping together. That is a great enrichment of married life and means that in man (as opposed to animals) physical sex is more surely in a context of love than it would otherwise be. We do not mate just like animals. We 'make *love*' before we sleep together. But it also means that if we go too far along the reaction chain it becomes deeply dissatisfying to stop short. It is not meant to satisfy us but to drive us on. Beyond a certain stage – certainly when any 'heavy petting' is involved – it is therefore a frustrating and emotionally exhausting business. This is true even for engaged couples. Engagement is not a certification of freedom here. It is just plain stupid to go so far that it is exceedingly difficult to stop. We must respect our make-up and not keep driving it into situations of overstrain. Petting, therefore, can never be an end in itself. Outside marriage it needs a tight rein because it is naturally part of a wider whole, and we have not got there yet.

If we have already gone too far there are two possible courses of action. It is easy to give up the fight for discipline and say to ourselves that we may as well be hung for a sheep as a lamb. We have overdone it, so does it matter if we go further? But that is a false argument and means a moral defeat. It is also likely to affect

47

our future relationships in really destructive ways. On the other hand we can discuss it frankly, confess to one another that it has been a mistake and agree to go back several stages and draw a line. Then we know where we are. Self-discipline of this kind will help us to grow in respect and understanding of one another's psychology (and physiology), and that is a necessary element in any life-long relationship. If we can get it all back in balance, this will allow the friendship to grow in a more healthy way.

Before closing this chapter let us notice a peculiar psychological trick that we tend to play. If one partner has in a previous relationship gone too far, and has a sense of guilt about it, he or she can be unreasonably keen to go that far again so as to feel that the new partner is now equal. It is like the drug addict who desperately wants others to take drugs, partly so that he shall no longer feel an outsider. The fellowship of sinners is sometimes more attractive than the fellowship of saints. Usually this is not altogether a conscious aim, but it means that any past excesses must be a special ground for caution. In any case that most unpopular virtue, self-control, is one of the marks of the Christian (it is one of the fruits of the Spirit, Galatians 5:23 and see 2 Timothy 1:7). There are few clearer proofs of spiritual and personal childishness than an inability to maintain self-control in such a matter. It is not adult or manly or womanly to be undisciplined here. It is plainly to behave like spoilt children who grab at anything they find attractive.

This brings us back to the start of this chapter. Short of marriage 'heavy' petting is a snare and a destructive

48

delusion. Short of engagement or really serious love very little physical demonstration is other than distracting from the growth of true love and friendship. Short of love almost all physical expression of love is a dangerous hypocrisy which is likely really to hurt someone. This is simply because we are physiologically and psychologically made in a certain way. What we stir up easily we cannot easily calm down. Physical excitement always tends to ask for more. The whole process is something which must excite our admiration and gratefulness to God, but we must not grasp after gifts which we cannot use or they will go rotten on us and spoil our relationships with God and with men.

4 An example of victory

No BOOK CAN compare with the Bible for sheer frankness. And no book handles such delicate subjects as this so tersely and without squeamishness. In Genesis 39 for example, is the story of how a young man met the seductions of an immoral woman, and with everything against him except God, chose slander and imprisonment rather than lose his honour and live with an unhappy conscience.

'And after a time his master's wife cast her eyes upon Joseph, and said, "Lie with me." But he refused and said to his master's wife, "Lo, having me my master has no concern about anything in the house, and he has put everything that he has in my hand; he is not greater in this house than I am; nor has he kept back anything from me except yourself, because you are his wife; how then can I do this great wickedness, and sin against God?" And although she spoke to Joseph day after day, he would not listen to her, to lie with her or to be

with her. But one day, when he went into the house to
do his work and none of the men of the house was there
in the house, she caught him by his garment, saying,
"Lie with me." But he left his garment in her hand, and
fled and got out of the house' (Genesis 39 : 7–12).

THE CIRCUMSTANCES OF THE TEMPTATION

At the age of seventeen, Joseph had been cruelly sold by
his brothers to some merchants. About ten years had
passed, during which he had patiently suffered the life
of a slave in Egypt, cut off completely from home and
friends, among a strange people, learning new customs
and speech, with no signs of redress nor prospect of freedom. He was, moreover, a bachelor, with little hope of
ever having a home and family of his own.

The temptation was remarkable for its *timing*. Joseph
was enjoying a welcome period of comparative ease.
God's presence had prospered him with the result that
his observant master, Potiphar, had put everything into
Joseph's capable hands, making him overseer of his
house and keeping no check on Joseph's activities. How
easily Joseph could have lowered his standards, grown
slack, and compromised with sin !

The *suddenness* of the temptation is also emphasized.
One day, without warning, Potiphar's wife made a
direct appeal to him with her looks and her words. If
Joseph had been indulging in impure thinking, he
would have been overcome as by a sudden squall from
an unexpected quarter. Many have been amazed and
ashamed at the lengths to which they could go on the
spur of the moment.

The temptation was striking also for its *subtlety*. To

please his master's wife might have had favourable results with his master himself. Most people regard it as expedient to stand well with the boss's wife if she is around. It must have been very difficult to offend and disappoint Potiphar's wife, seeing she had much influence with his master. She could easily get him into trouble.

The temptation was accompanied also by *persistency*. She spoke to Joseph, not once or twice only, but day after day. If some people's resistance is overcome by suddenness, that of others is worn down slowly by the steady continuance of the attack.

Look, also, at the *opportunity* for the temptation. 'None of the men of the house was there in the house.' There was no-one to see and no-one would ever find out. Potiphar's wife would never dream of telling of her own sin. Joseph could win her favour without incurring anyone's censure.

THE CONQUEST OF THE TEMPTATION

Joseph never regarded sensual indulgence as a necessity. Nothing can so undermine resistance to temptation as the fantastic notion that restraint of this kind is unhealthy. When the psychologist talks about repression, he does not mean conscious, wilful resistance; he means the refusal to think about a thing by repressing it into the unconscious mind. And that is just what people do who give way to sin. They have to repress a sense of shame, and do their best to forget God, who knows and sees everything. In the attack on the city of Mansoul in Bunyan's *Holy War*, it was when Mr Resistance was knocked off the wall that the enemy came in.

The will must be strengthened by a right mental attitude.

Joseph called the thing by its proper name – not 'being a little fast' or 'having a gay time' or 'sowing wild oats', but 'this great wickedness' and 'sin against God'.

Joseph also put a proper estimate on it: 'this *great* wickedness', he called it. And it does not become any less great for becoming more common, or for being accompanied by measures to reduce the risk of physical consequences.

Above all, he judged it in the light of God. Potiphar's wife thought no-one could see: she would not have dreamed of doing such a thing in the presence of her husband, but she had no fear of God in her heart. Joseph saw it as a sin against God, who, it says, was with him. The presence of God was more real to Joseph than that of any earthly master. He knew it would break his enjoyment of God's presence, and that he would one day have to give account to Him.

Joseph was very wise in taking reasonable precautions, refusing not only to give way to her, but also to listen to her, or even to be with her. He met the temptation at an early stage, keeping it at the circumference of his life, instead of fighting it when it reached the centre.

The best place to win the battle for chastity is in the earliest stages, in fact, in the thoughts. We must take reasonable precautions to avoid the things and places and people which excite impure thoughts: certain books, magazines, films, advertisements, many forms of dancing and scanty dress. Some may despise this as puritanical, but it is a miserable business to be indifferent to the enemy's piercing the outer ring of defences, and so let him get to closer grips with you. No-one can avoid the temptation of a momentary lustful thought or impulse, but then is the time to refuse to welcome it and lick it over, and to think instead on good and wholesome things.

We really can be incredibly stupid and can easily place ourselves under totally unnecessary strains. When the car broke down for a courting couple recently, and the only place where they could spend the night offered only a double bedroom, it really was not necessary to accept, saying that of course they would be self-controlled! He could, and should, have slept in the lounge. And the car itself can be a menace if we allow it to be. Sitting hunched up in the dark with room and light for nothing but petting, we are mad if we think we can spend our evenings together that way without its putting a tremendous strain on us. If we know that drink leads to death on the roads, we surely know that equally easily it leads to the death of uprightness because we lose adequate control. Joseph's world was different from ours, but he took the necessary precautions to avoid high-pressure temptation as far as he could: that in itself represented an attitude to evil. Some of us live as if we really hope to be so overwhelmingly tempted that we can sin with some shade of excuse! We do not hate sin as Joseph did.

In spite of his precautions, however, Joseph found himself in a position in which brief hesitation might have been disastrous. And it was due to the habit of living a disciplined life that *he did not hesitate at the critical moment.* 'He left his garment in her hand, and fled and got out of the house.' The battle was won.

God does not always reward the righteous immediately. Joseph was called to suffer terribly for righteousness' sake. Before his master and all the men of the house, Potiphar's wife accused him of the very sin of which she had been so guilty, and Joseph was flung, in disgrace, into what may literally be translated 'The Hole'. Used to the freedom of the plains, his spirit must have suffered deeply as, bound with chains, misunderstood, misrepresented and falsely accused, he shared that dark, damp, small and badly ventilated cell with the king's special political prisoners.

But that was not the end of the story. How could it be? The Lord was with him and, though unknown to himself at the time, was turning his imprisonment into a two-year training course for future work of first importance. How glad Joseph must have been in the end that he did not give way! If he had done, he would have remained in Potiphar's palace, would never have been promoted to second in command of all Egypt, never have earned the gratitude of millions whom he saved in the famine, never have seen his father and brothers again; and, above all, a cloud would have come between himself and God together with deep bewilderment as to how it could be removed.

5 What if we fail?

MANY PEOPLE HAVE past experiences which they would rather not remember. Some Christians are acutely aware of failures in the past or the present which tempt them to give up and regard it as no longer important to try. None of us can be complacent or self-righteous in this area and when we remember our Lord's words about the lustful thought constituting 'adultery in the heart' we may be inclined to despair. If we have lost our virginity of mind or body we may ask (or the devil may ask us), 'Does anything else matter? Had we not better give up the struggle or at least lower our ideals and cease to care for the very high standards of the New Testament?'

Perhaps the best answer of the Bible to this problem is contained in its biographies. David, of all people – the man whose Psalms are still unequalled as expressions of praise and devotion to God – David failed in this area. At a time when he was over-relaxing (he should have

57

been out with the army) he was tempted and fell. The history traces out the tragic consequences of his adultery with Bathsheba. His sons began to follow their father's example. Amnon raped his half-sister and this led on to murder and finally to the rebellion of Absalom and to the public humiliation of David's wives. This, he was told explicitly, was a consequence of his immorality.

Yet David's relationship to God was restored before very long. His Psalm 51 is unequalled as a prayer of penitence and the acceptance of undeserved forgiveness. He was brought back to fellowship with God and to usefulness in God's service and even to his greatest of all contributions – the writing of Psalms. His failure was abject and total. He was even led by it to the murder of Bathsheba's husband. But he was not irrevocably rejected by God. If he had given up and become a licentious man, not only he and his kingdom and his family would have suffered far worse, but the church of God all down the ages would have been impoverished. Yet he never altogether escaped the consequences of his sin in his family and his country. Things were never the same again. Tragedy struck and most of it was directly attributable to the consequences of his sin.

This is the pattern of biblical teaching in the matter. Whatever our sins, they can be totally forgiven by God without any possibility of recall. 'Thou hast cast all my sins behind thy back' (Isaiah 38 : 17). They are 'cast into the depths of the sea' (Micah 7 : 19). If God, as He says, forgets them (Isaiah 43 : 25), so should we. To be justified by faith in Christ is, as the children's illustration has it, to be 'just-as-if-I'd' never sinned before God.

In a comprehensive sense, however, we cannot be just as if we had never sinned. Sin has its consquences and we shall have to accept them. These we cannot escape even though we are forgiven, and we must learn to live with them as David did. It must not cloud our relationship to God or discourage our determination not to be defeated again. It must not crush us or discourage us from seeking God's very best. Indeed the consequences of sin should be a constant warning and deterrent to us. But in rejoicing in a total and undeserved restoration to God we must be humbled by the reminder of the fact that we have messed up God's creation and abused His gifts, and we may find the path to God's very best for us much more difficult. Of course what God gives us is His best. No-one should think of himself as now in a second-class category. All God's children are privileged objects of His perfect care and continual grace and gifts. We always have far more than we deserve and are given tasks to do for God for which we are ourselves entirely unworthy. So David prays in Psalm 51: 'Restore to me the joy of thy salvation, and uphold me with a willing spirit. *Then* I will teach transgressors thy ways, and sinners will return to thee . . . O Lord, open thou my lips, and my mouth shall show forth thy praise.' This prayer was answered. He lived to praise and serve God and to turn others to faith. So may we.

Samson is also a marvellous, if frightening, example of the same kind of experience. He was magnificent in physical stature and appearance; a national hero and leader, a military commander of ability, appointed by God to deliver the nation from their oppressors. God's special blessings of physical strength and providential control in battle rested on him. He had seen exceptional and miraculous answers to prayer. But he was pathetically weak in his affections. He could fight others, but had no control over himself. In spite of warnings and protests by others, he drifted progressively into a licentious life of disobedience to God in immoral relationships with pagan girls.

It ended up, of course, in tragedy. But for a long time Samson seems to have carried on regardless, perhaps because God's gifts of strength and leadership continued to rest on him. When he was deeply involved in evil – sleeping with a pagan prostitute in Gaza – he still had supernatural strength by which he escaped from apparently certain death at the hands of the Philistines.

Perhaps this made him careless. Perhaps he felt that God obviously did not mind very much because His power was still given to him. We do not know. Many lesser Christian leaders have hushed up their conscience in this way because, for the sake of the church, God has continued to use them in various ways for good. What should have humbled them and driven them to repentance has been turned to make them reckless of evil in their own lives. But it cannot last long.

In the end he gave away everything to a girl who was a complete sham – a spy who pretended to love him, for the sake of her country and financial reward. And he was so infatuated he could not see it. She sold her body for her country and her idols, and he sold his country and his God for the sake of his sexual appetite.

Of the two she was the more noble; but she was un-principled, and he had lost his power of real friendship and discrimination. His sin found him out. She let him down; he lost his strength and his leadership and ended up in prison with his eyes put out and doing the task of a mule.

We are given no glimpses of his state of mind in pri-son, but from what follows we can be pretty sure that he was brought to his senses at last. He had betrayed his people and failed to deliver them as God had intended. He had pursued so-called 'love' improperly and had been rewarded with commercial trickery. He was the laughing-stock of the world and had discredited the name of God.

But God had not deserted Samson. It seems clear that he was forgiven and restored to God. He grew his hair again and this was the outward sign of a vow of un-qualified service to God. That, of course, did not give him back his sight or his freedom. He lived with these consequences of his sin until his death. But God still had a job for him to do and when the opportunity came, at a celebration of the superior power of the Philistine god Dagon, God, the living God of Israel, gave to Samson the final opportunity to show that Dagon was nothing and to strike his most powerful blow yet for the freedom of his nation.

Here is both a warning and an encouragement. Sam-son had sunk so low that one might have thought that God could never give him another task to do again. But that would be quite wrong. True, he could never again be an accepted and trusted leader of his people. What he did had to be done in another way. No-one in Israel could have had any more confidence in him as an official representative. But God's mercy remained. God heard his prayers, and God still had mighty things for him to do. Since the coming of Christ, we know God's love in far greater measure and in far clearer ways. No matter how we may have failed in the past, and no matter how we may be forced to live with the consequences of our failure, we must rejoice in God's total forgiveness and His perfect plan for us to enjoy His unclouded fellowship. What is more, we must believe that God has a job for us to do still. It may not be the same job as before, but no God-given task is ever a second best. It is always the highest honour possible.

The biblical picture leads us, therefore, to this double attitude to past failure. First, an acceptance of the fact that it may spoil good things on the human level and rob us of the opportunity of serving God in certain ways. But second, we have to take this as a warning to avoid sin now and in the future, and go on to enjoy God's unclouded fellowship through the death of Christ for our sins. That means that we never give up. We get up, if we have fallen, and by God's grace and strength look for fresh ways of serving Him and living a life that is pleasing to Him.

In certain situations there may even be an opportunity to retrace our steps, and to put right what is wrong. Some who read this book may have realized for the first time that their present situation is quite contrary to God's will. They may be living with someone to whom they are not married, or engaged to someone, perhaps a non-Christian, whom they now know in their hearts they should not wed. The big battle is to find the courage to admit the mistake and to extricate oneself from it.

In such circumstances the temptation to let things slide must be overcome. We shall almost certainly need the help of Christian friends in whom we can confide, whose judgment we respect, and who will help us to find the strength needed to do what is right. Just as those who are trying to break their dependence on drugs may suffer physically from withdrawal symptoms, so there may be a period of loneliness and depression following our decision to break with the past, during which the understanding support of fellow-Christians will be essential. Doing the right thing may not leave us with unclouded psychological peace and joy, although it will restore us to God's fellowship and bring back our peace with Him. And that is what really matters. We shall have to accept what really cannot be remedied. But we must not use that as an excuse for not tackling the things that can still be put right or at least could be vastly improved. The ideal may now be beyond recovery, but we can, and must, fight for the best that is open to us. God wants the best for us. We should want it too.

6 Are Christian morals unalterable?

How COULD ANY moral precepts, enunciated a long time ago, be still equally authoritative and binding upon us now? Times have changed. New moral choices are before us and the same old actions now have different consequences. Contraception is a case in point.

First let us look at what sort of thing Christian morality is. It is not given us in the Bible as a complete set of rules or a detailed programme of do's and don'ts. For the most part Christian morality consists of a few basic principles whose detailed application is left to the Christian.

There are, on the other hand, a few fixed points or *rules* – things which are always evil, such as murder and adultery. Even these, as Jesus made plain in the Sermon on the Mount, are particular, practical, black and white examples of broader principles. They are not the main thing. Far from exhausting morality, they show what kind of thing morality is and what much wider responsibilities we have.

The case of murder makes it clear. This was forbidden in the Ten Commandments. In the Sermon on the Mount Jesus taught that this does not just mean 'no murder', but that hatred and violent abuse and whatever else tends to the same result is wrong. We cannot congratulate ourselves on not being murderers if we are ruled by hatred. But equally we cannot excuse murder on the grounds that we did it without hate. Murder, it is explained, is in an absolute sense an evil. It is not allowed to us to take another man's life, because life in a special sense belongs to God. Murder was absolutely forbidden as well as the emotions and words that are likely to lead to it. How this works out in practice was not further elaborated in the New Testament. Hatred is often denounced and love demanded, but apart from one or two commands about bad temper and swearing, and these are also general, that is it! We are expected to think it out in the Christian community and try to arrive at such practical rules as are necessary, or such guides to personal conscience as will help us in times of temptation, when we shall want to rationalize our selfish desires.

The same sort of situation obtains with regard to the other Ten Commandments. 'Thou shalt not steal' is in the Old Testament a particular case of the larger principle of justice. 'Thou shalt not bear false witness' is a particular case of a principle of truth, and 'Thou shalt not commit adultery' is a particular case of the principle of marital fidelity. These particular cases illustrate the principles in a pure, crystalline form. They were binding rules for the Hebrew society and the New

Testament accepts them as binding too, though it emphasizes also that they are only the bare bones of morality and that love is the goal and fulfilment of these laws.[1]

It is really very impressive how the apostle Paul refuses to be pinned down to a lot of detailed rules in the matter of sex morality. In 1 Corinthians 7, for instance, he keeps referring us to the relevant principles. Each has to find a vocation from God; marriage is sacrosanct and sexual intercourse is to be confined to marriage; Christians are to marry only Christians; whether married or single we are to be unselfish and to put God's service first.[2] This really is extremely helpful and practical, although it hardly descends to details at all. In several cases where it seems he was asked a precise question he refused to give a yes or no answer, but refers them to principles.

The principles are absolute and unchangeable because they are related to the way we are made. For the same reason they apply equally to all men, whether they are Christians or not. All are created beings living in God's created world, and all ought to keep His rules for their life and will find them by far the best. Christian morality is never arbitrary or alien to man's nature. It is tailor-made for him. To take a familiar example, in Ephesians 4 Paul says: 'Putting away falsehood, let every one speak the truth with his neighbour, for we are members one of another.' The principle is truth; the reason is that all breaches of the principle are an offence against the fact that we are 'members one of another'. Now this last point is unalterable because it is a matter

[1] See, for example, Romans 13.
[2] For a detailed study of this chapter see Chapter 9.

of the way in which society works. We live in society, and society depends for its healthy functioning on some degree of trust and mutual reliability. To lie is to erode this basis of society. That is a rule arising out of the principle and exemplifying it. But that leaves us with an enormous area of practical application to work out for ourselves.

To return, then, to our original question : How can any ancient moral precepts still be authoritative? Our answer is as follows. The biblical moral precepts are mainly basic moral principles, based on the way we are made. They are therefore unalterable, as the principle of truth is unalterable. To lie always injures relationships, even if only remotely. Every act of adultery is another blow against the stability of marriage and of the family. To commit fornication is, according to the Bible, to sin again the *body* (1 Corinthians 6); it is always an insult and injury to the body. It is not a question of relative customs because it goes down to the basic way in which we are made, rather as potassium cyanide always kills because it stops a basic biochemical reaction on which all life depends. Some acts are as inevitably harmful as taking some poisons, because man's human nature doesn't change. This refers partly to the body, but even more to man's psychological make-up. Sexual intercourse makes the partners one in a unique sense; therefore to indulge in it in the wrong context is evil. The Bible tells us that it is only within marriage that it is in context, and therefore good and health-giving rather than evil and a sin against the body. That is not a question of custom or culture, but of how we are made. Both the principles and the few fixed points of application of principles given in the Bible are therefore permanent.

Beyond these, however, there are few if any unalterable rules. Customs do change, as those who travel abroad soon discover. For a woman to dress in a certain way may be widely acceptable in Britain; but when she visits a Muslim country and does the same, people are led to assume that she is an immoral person. Certainly it stimulates erotic ideas in the minds of the spectators, as their comments make clear. Apart from the need to consider others and to cause no stumbling to them, there is no detailed rule about dress (in 1 Timothy 2 : 9 the instruction is to be 'modest' and that, within limits, means different things in different cultures). Similarly, when Paul is asked about meat offered to idols, he refuses to give a neat answer because there is nothing wrong with the meat in itself. All depends on what it means to others. Many of our customs with regard to sex and marriage (*e.g.* a considerable period of firm engagement before marriage) have no definite biblical authority, but are merely extremely wise, practical conventions. If we exalt all of these into unalterable rules we shall soon find that life is impossible, and we shall easily lose sight of the biblical fixed points, which are the ones that really matter.

The Christian can be sure, therefore, that what is specifically commanded or forbidden in the New Testament is permanent if it is a principle or a particular application of a principle. There can be only two situations where we do not accept biblical commands as literally binding on us always. The first is relatively rare; it is where the customs to which it refers simply do not mean the same thing today. To interpret the instruction to 'greet one another with a holy kiss' literally is bound today to lead to trouble, or shall we say that in our times it is too difficult! John Bunyan observed that the kiss of the elders after church did not seem to him always to be holy. The attractive women were kissed with an unholy enthusiasm by some and the practice had to be replaced by a greeting which *fully expressed the principle* in another way. In any case, of course, the command was not described as a moral command at all.

The other situation is where we can really satisfy our consciences that an exceptional path is absolutely *necessary* to prevent some far greater evil. There are exceptions in the matter of truth (*e.g.* in wartime). Then we shall have to think it out and perhaps deliberately decide that in certain situations to lie is the lesser evil of the choices open to us. The same is true about killing in wartime. Lesser evil choices do arise, especially where sin has messed things up. Where a couple have divorced and each married again and had children there is no clear-cut solution if one or both becomes a Christian.

Morality has some parallels with driving a car. If there were no rules of the road travel would be nearly impossible. Some are just good conventions, but there are also things that you must not do because the car has physical limitations. There are things you must not do because of what we may call 'creation limits'. For instance, almost every country has a limit in built-up areas of about the same speed, because it is related to the driver's and pedestrian's reaction times. It is only a rule; but it has to be almost the same everywhere and everyone has to respect it. Only if they do so do they have freedom on the roads. The principle is to con-

70

sider the other man and the limits of your machine (brakes in particular!). The rule is 30 m.p.h. That in itself, however, does not make a good driver. A man who merely keeps the rules can be so infuriating to others that he tempts them to disaster. Driving is no more a matter of merely keeping within the rules than is Christian morality. The good driver keeps the rules but he is in more subtle ways no danger to others, gets to his destination pretty fast and to the pleasure of his passengers. But these are merely negative aspects to good driving and some of them pretty basic.

Nevertheless there are crises in which the driver will steer into the ditch, exceed the speed limit or even deliberately smash up his car to avoid a worse accident. He will have to justify what he did in court, if it broke the rules, and he may be able to convince the magistrates that it was the lesser of a choice between two evils. If something far worse was inevitable, and only then, he would probably be excused.

Man is not infinitely adaptable. There are things that we cannot do to him or with him without irreversible damage. Society is even more sensitive and we cannot ignore the fact that we live in society and many things are not worth doing unless at least one other person can be persuaded to do them with us.

God has given us both the principles and a few rules. Breaches of the rules have to be justified to God, not just to men, and a merely selfish justification – 'it seemed so natural' – will not suffice. No-one has yet been able to think of a situation in which we would be clearly justified in committing adultery as the lesser evil. There may be exceptions to *some* of the other Ten

71

Commandments, but it happens that in this case it is apparently impossible to find one.

In the area of sexual morality, therefore, things are clear. God gives us guide lines. But a courtship that merely kept within certain limits would be, to put it mildly, pretty tame. God does not want us *merely* to keep within limits. He wants us to love with a quality of love that is truly unselfish, truly human and stable enough to last for life. We need enough rules to give us safety with freedom. This is exactly what God gives us. He made us, He loves us, and He knows. He also commands for our good.

7 Prelude to partnership

It has often been pointed out that the Bible mentions two, and only two, relations between Christian men and women: brothers and sisters in Christ, or husband and wife. If to this notably brief list we add the reasonably in-between state of being about-to-get-married, then the problem confronting the Christian is this: How do I pass from being the brother or sister of all my brethren to being the husband or wife of one of them?

In negotiating this difficult passage, the Christian has the immense advantage of divine guidance, here as at all times. For the average person, the risk of choosing the wrong man or woman to be husband or wife is considerable. For the Christian the risk is far smaller, but it is by no means eliminated. Even among Christians, mistakes occur. Some of these mistakes end in unwise and unsatisfactory marriages. Others are caught in time. But their end product is a bitter taste in the mouths of the two people concerned, a loss of confidence and openness, and damage to the reputation of God's people among those who look on.

CAUSES OF DISCONTENT

Many of these mistakes stem from unsatisfactory beginnings to friendships at college and university; the relationships get off to a bad start, and it is with these beginnings that we are now concerned, for the golden rule in all such friendships is to start as you mean to go on.

Why are some friendships between Christians unsatisfactory and, ultimately, damaging? Some common reasons for bad beginnings are, first, that nearly every student has a girl friend or boy friend, so why be left out? Men students feel that it is expected of them to take a girl out, and girl students wish that they had someone to 'phone them up and take them out as the other girls have. It thus becomes in the *mores* of student life more proper to be 'going steady' than either to be a free-lance or not to be 'going' at all.

Secondly, Christian students often form attachments on the basis of a common interest in spiritual things and in these alone, forgetting that marriage involves the body and the mind as well, in fact the whole person, and is essentially a very human and down-to-earth matter. If they forget this they are no better off than Pierre Daninos' Major Thompson, who said of his fox-hunting wife that 'we were not so much united by love as reconciled to each other by a common passion for horses'.

To share a common interest in Sunday School work is not, in itself, a decisive indicator that you should get married. Far less is the (evidently fatal) attraction of

74

having served together on a Christian committee. As someone remarked, some men marry girls who would make excellent curates when what they need is a wife.

A special case of this one-sided relationship is the friendship that consists of writing letters to each other on spiritual topics; personal remarks are excluded, and the correspondence is simply a kind of fellowship-by-post. Of this it is perhaps enough to say that the statistics are clear; such friendships always end in one of two things – frustration or marriage.

Thirdly, men have a tendency to over-commit themselves in the early stages of friendships, and later find that, as in a revolving door, they are backing out again while the girl is just getting in. This over-commitment is commonly the result of two errors. One is the habit men have of acting too soon to 'cut out of the herd' the girl of their choice. This they do, as they will tell you, to be able to get to know her and so make up their minds. But to the girl it seems as if they have made up their minds already. The other is a male habit of letting the hands get ahead of either the heart or mind. Men will often begin holding hands or putting their arm round a girl quite casually and then profess to be taken aback when the girl reads into their actions anything more than a friendly gesture.

Finally, some of these friendships are unsatisfactory because they proceed for too long without any clear expression of intention on the man's part. If the girl asks for a clear statement, he contrives to make her sound forward; if she does not, he may let her risk her happiness – not to speak of wasting her time – only to find in the end that he did not 'intend' anything, and would think it unspiritual to have done so.

SOME PRACTICAL SUGGESTIONS

These are some of the hazards to be negotiated, and forewarned is forearmed. But can we not avoid the hazards altogether? To attempt to make rules about courting would be extremely rash, but there are a few simple suggestions that can be offered.

In the first place, at the beginning of friendships, you should proceed by group activities rather than *tête à tête*. In this respect, college life offers excellent opportunities for men and girls to meet and observe each other under a wide variety of conditions. (Contrast, for example, the problem of choice of a young couple who work in different offices or factories, and have nowhere to go in the evenings but to the pictures.) Girls, in any case, often resent being singled out too obviously, and many a promising friendship has been damaged by an over-prompt invitation to tea for two.

The second suggestion is more specifically for Christians. It is that, in courting, our Christian standards may require us to forgo some of the thrills of the chase, as they are formulated by Hollywood and the popular press. To keep two men – or more if she can – dangling is one of the recognized prerogatives of the female, but this gratifying pastime is non-Christian. There is no more damaging person in a college than a Christian girl who is known in the student world in general as a flirt – unless it be a woman-chasing man student. The first requirement in Christian courtship is honesty – even if this means, as it probably will, that instead of keeping his girl friend in delicious suspense waiting for the One Big Question, a Christian man gives her an indication of what is in his mind and so affords the opportunity of praying about it.

Let it be added at once that this does not mean, as some Christians seem to think, that it is unspiritual to be in love or to say so. Sometimes a Christian man will go up to a girl and say, 'I feel it is the Lord's will that I should marry you.' This leaves the girl in an appalling dilemma! Does he love her, or is he doing this from a sense of duty? Does the fact that she happens to find him repulsive merely mean that she has missed the guidance or is unspiritual? Here, we can propound one rule which is completely safe: if he says that, and does not also say that he loves you, turn him down!

The third suggestion is that if, like most people, you have a mental checklist of what you want in a life-partner, you should keep it short, and use it not so much to assess everyone you meet as a potential wife or husband, but in order to exclude those who obviously are not. The Christian's choice is, or should be, severely limited by the fact that the first two questions on his checklist are: (1) Is she (he) a Christian, and (2) What sort of a Christian is she (he)? This means that there are a large number of men or girls whom you can dismiss at once from your calculations. You should do so! It should be added that, human nature being what it is, we all too commonly find that a Christian man meets an attractive non-Christian girl, and says to himself, 'If she were a Christian I should like her for a wife.' So he appoints himself evangelist to her, in the hope that one day she will be converted, when, in gratitude to him, she will tend naturally to fall straight into his arms. But the statistics triumph again; it almost never happens, and where this is the initial motive, the girl is extremely unlikely to become a genuine Christian.

'What sort of a Christian?' It is not a question, of course, of activity or Bible knowledge, although those might be indicators. Jim Elliot, the martyr-missionary of Ecuador, whose credentials in this matter are beyond dispute, used a phrase in describing his future wife which exactly defines the Christian's ideal. She had, he said, 'an immense hunger for God'.

By contrast with these first two, the other questions on your checklist are likely to be unimportant. She may not like Beethoven, or she may be blonde whereas you require a brunette. But God has a way of over-fulfilling our requirements nonetheless. All the other questions, indeed, can be eliminated except one, and for the Christian this is a vital test : 'Is she (he) a person whom I can enjoy as a friend and rely on as a helper?' The early years of Christian marriage do not consist of prayer and Bible study, but mainly of noisy children and disturbed nights. We must never allow our spiritual assessments to blind us to the fact that, for the present, we are in the body. The basis of marriage must be true friendship and this needs to be tested by doing ordinary things together, ideally in the company of others.

We must remember what marriage is – a lifelong friendship and partnership which will suffer numerous stresses and strains. Spiritual unity is essential and must come first with an absolute priority, but we are talking about a human relationship. Sadly one has met a few Christian couples whose marriages have been exceedingly difficult, or even have broken up, where the reason appears to be that they thought only in spiritual terms. A Christian can be so relieved to find a fellow-Christian of like mind and spirit who responds to preliminary 'feelers' that they rush into marriage without asking carefully whether they are really able to make an excellent human relationship of it. The advice of parents and friends is important. All marriages have their problems and are the richer for these problems once they have been overcome. But we are not infinitely adaptable. We cannot ignore the particular human characteristics that God has given us, and we must be sure that our differences can be made constructively stimulating and not destructively abrasive.

The fourth and last suggestion concerns not the principles in the friendship, but the onlookers. Mankind has an inveterate tendency towards matrimony – in other people. Compared with the casual and cynical world outside (which has long since discarded the public-school aphorism that only a cad would tamper with a girl's affections), the Christian is often extraordinarily naïve about friendships; he (or, more usually, she) cannot see one without wanting to promote it to its triumphant conclusion. All too often, this pressure from the rear pushes a couple along more rapidly than they intend and denies them their undoubted freedom to take their own time to be sure.

In this respect, and whatever its other drawbacks, the American system of casual dates – the recognized principle of which is that keeping the date does not commit either party – has a good deal to be said for it. Let us be mature about this, and let us remember that, unless we are asked to intervene or have some special responsibility, the standard Christian way of 'helping' is by prayer, not by setting man-traps.

Marriage was ordained by God; men and women are given to each other for their mutual comfort and help; celibacy is not an ultimate Christian ideal, even though we may be clear that it is our calling for the next few years. Still less of a Christian ideal is rudeness to the opposite sex. It is possible to be polite, friendly and 'outgoing' without becoming involved in thoughts of matrimony. So often Christian girl students complain that the Christian men will not speak to them, much less take part in any social activity; so they accept invitations from the non-Christian men. This is a matter for our attention. On the other hand courtship is a very time-consuming and distracting business. There are stages in life when we can ill afford the extra burden on our time and energies. We must ask ourselves whether at present we can possibly take it on. Many overseas students deliberately refuse to get involved because they know that they will fail exams if they do. The Christian must ask himself what are his present priorities.

For most Christians, the years at college offer more spare time than any subsequent period. On the other hand, they are very often years of exceptionally rapid spiritual movement; God seems to use them to do things to us quickly, before we settle down in life. Therefore there is a case for saying, 'In these years I shall let nothing, bad or good, prejudice my devoting my whole attention to learning what God has to teach me.' But let us not forget Paul's saving injunction, 'Let every one lead the life which the Lord has assigned to him, and in which God has called him' (1 Corinthians 7 : 17). While it is improbable that you meet your future partner in your first year at university, and not even likely that you will meet him or her in your last, nevertheless it is entirely possible that God will so plan for you. Let us learn to trust the Holy Spirit in one another.

8 Is early marriage the answer?

To MANY PEOPLE the simple solution of all the problems of sex is to get married. Indeed Paul seems to argue that way in 1 Corinthians 7 : 1-7. If we are the sort of people who cannot settle down happily to a single life, then 'each man should have his own wife and each woman her own husband'. Add to this the fear of both men and women of being left out – on the shelf – or finding ourselves not masculine (or feminine) enough to make a good partner, and the pressure is on to get married quickly and to believe that the problems that follow will be small and can be taken in their stride.

In fact, however, the Bible gives a lot of space to the problems that arise in Christian marriages. If we rush into marriage without solving our problems of personality and our problems of sex it is likely that we shall simply work them off on our partner, and that can be a very destructive process. All of us have visited homes where husband and wife were obviously not well adjusted or were even showing signs of distressing friction. Marriages, even those between Christians, are nowadays much more frequently ending up in divorce, and that warns us that all is not well with the common attitudes of people towards getting married today.

MOTIVES

The first question to ask is, why do we want to get married? Is it purely selfish? No-one should pretend that no selfish elements enter into it. Sexual love is like that; it wants to possess, it calls out for satisfaction. But is that all? Marriage is nowadays also a status symbol, rather like a Ph.D. Ordinary students have their boy friends and girl friends; the married student has 'arrived' and is looked upon with a certain envy and respect. There is a feeling that if we can achieve marriage we really are grown up and have got somewhere. Chapter 9 of this book is to some extent an answer to that.

To others marriage is the only solution in sight to the so-called identity crisis. Since they left home and school some students are acutely aware that they are socially adrift; they belong to no-one. There is a very natural and not in itself un-wholesome desire to belong, to be someone, to be of significance to at least one other person. This makes it extremely desirable to have a partner, and when that proves a bit superficial we hope that marriage (or sleeping with our partner before marriage) will somehow do the trick. But the idea is to solve *my* problem; I want to get married not because I love someone, but because I feel psychologically deprived. My partner is a mere means to an end and the result is the most unsatisfactory relationship possible.

82

Motives for marriage are no doubt extremely mixed. No-one can possibly decide the matter for anyone else and dogmatically approve or disapprove. But we can and should ask in particular, what is the quality of our love? Is there in addition to sexual attraction a genuinely unselfish love which longs to serve the other, to help him or her to growth and increased usefulness to men and to God?

The author had a sad discussion not long ago with a former Christian Union leader. He had married another member of the CU and they now had a family. He said that they were in such constant friction at home that he had decided to go and live in a flat alone, leaving his wife with the children. He went home only occasionally and even so, the visit was never happy. Pressed as to the reason for the breakdown he said that, as far as he could see, they had never been well suited to each other. Having a very limited experience of life and people, and knowing that they wanted to marry only a Christian, they had paired off in the CU and decided to get married quickly without any adequate thought as to what was involved. Almost immediately they had run into trouble, because the human factors were so against them and they had been too proud to seek help from any experienced friends. In a recent survey almost a quarter of the wives said they felt they had married too early. There are big human adjustments to make and a starry-eyed idealism does not help us very much in making them.

Some people do really fall deeply in love after marrying for largely selfish reasons, but it is, to put it mildly, tempting providence to ask that marriage will work that miracle in us. Marriage is a wonderful thing, but it brings none of its benefits automatically. It is intended by God to do us a lot of good, but it is not in the least likely by itself to make selfish people, who marry for selfish reasons, into thoroughly altruistic parents and partners.

CHARACTER

Basically the trouble is that marriage brings two still imperfect and sinful characters into an extremely close partnership. Either or both may then very soon be faced with quite new psychological strains and stresses (illness, loss of an interesting job, the worries of the rat-race, new responsibilities, sleepless nights and extreme tiredness, *etc.*). Both are also still growing up and facing the change from parent and peer-group (*e.g.* CU) dependence to a greater degree of isolation and mutual dependence. It is all frankly so new and brings such new demands that the weaknesses of our character are drawn out in a most disconcerting way. We find the person who prayed nicely and was very keen in spiritual things has a selfish view of the home. (His father always expected to be waited on like a king and so does he – that is partly why he married. Her mother spoiled her and never allowed her to help much in the house, and now all domestic chores are a maddening waste of time.) Perhaps he or she is an academic dreamer and infuriatingly unpractical – or just plain selfish, moody, unaffectionate or unthoughtful for others. Their character has never yet been tested and refined by much experience, and we had not expected to have to help them at these points. We shall probably also surprise even ourselves at times with our meanness and selfishness.

After all has been said about the wonders of sexual

attraction and love, it really takes some powerful forces to help two sinners to become truly one and to develop a rich partnership. It is marvellous how often marriage succeeds, thanks to these God-given instincts; but it is never altogether easy and many non-Christian marriages just break up in the first two years in disillusionment. The Christian is in a different position. He has the vastly greater cohesive force of a common faith and basic outlook. He has also the determination to make a success of the relationship whatever the problems. During the troubles of the first two years he will persevere in love and in prayer when others will give up. Our pride, for instance, can be very much hurt when difficulties arise. We always thought that we would make someone an ideal partner, and when it emerges that we do not, we can be very resentful against the one who has exposed our weakness. So marriage may be terribly demanding and humiliating and for that very reason it will be more enriching in the long run. But we have only to look around us to see that it may be quite difficult and very distressing, basically because our characters are still so imperfect. That will remain true whatever our motives were.

'NOT LIGHTLY'

That is not to belittle the great wonder of marriage. It is a tremendous gift of God to those who enter into it rightly. It is enormous fun, the greatest human adventure. Huge benefits come to the partners, their children and the community at large from wholesome marriages. But we are all too aware of the cruel evils that arise when it goes wrong. Like any other adventure it involves hard

85

preparation and periods of sheer grind. Supposing we join an expedition to the South Pole or the Upper Amazon. There will be times when we have to set our teeth and just keep plodding on. The glib agreement to go is severely tested and it is then that everyone sees whether we have what it takes to be a real 'adventurer', or whether we went out in a spirit of immature enthusiasm. The marriage service therefore, after all its positive emphases, rightly says that marriage must not be entered into 'unadvisedly, lightly or wantonly'.

Students are up against a special problem. While we are both still studying, marriage often seems easy and natural. But we have then only postponed the tremendous adjustments that we shall both have to make when we leave the student world and start doing a job. These will change us also and make entirely fresh demands upon us. The first year in the first job is for almost everyone pretty tough. It is also an experience that changes us almost as much as our first year as students. To marry while we are still studying, therefore, is to bring all the strains and stresses of these transitions into our marriage. To some extent it is marrying blind, because we have not yet experienced adult life and have both of us a lot of changes to go through.

Certain things need to be settled, therefore, before we think seriously of this lifelong commitment.

1. Am I ready to enter into such a demanding relationship? Am I too selfish? Am I able to put into practice the demands of Christian love as in 1 Corinthians 13, even when my partner is tired, unresponsive, selfish, irritable, critical or sick? How will my character stand up to it? Remember, marriage is 'for better for worse, for richer for poorer, in sickness and in health'!

2. What is the quality of my love for him or her? If there is any real doubt, has it been tested? What has happened when we have been separated for a long spell and what has happened when we have been together for a long spell? A friend once asked whether I thought that the fact that he and his fiancée had been together for sixteen hours and quarrelled for twelve of them was a good or bad sign! How do we get on in a home setting – preferably both his and hers? What happens under strain? Will our love be such as to triumph? The vow is 'to love and to cherish, till death us do part'.

3. What is the quality of our human relationship? Do we enjoy one another's interests and are the differences between us sources of friction or of pleasant stimulus? Are we really friends on a wide basis and able to enrich one another on a level of friendship? Do we really want to 'live together' (and not merely sleep together), and 'forsaking all others, keep only to him (her), so long as you both shall live'?

A friend of the author who was on the point of engagement came away from being best man at a wedding, wiping his brow and saying, 'Wow, I could never make all those promises.' It was at least a year more before he put the question and was accepted, and that year of waiting was pure gain.

4. What are our motives? That is, what are our motives for wanting to marry, for wanting to marry now and for wanting to marry this particular person?

These are all questions on which an experienced friend who knows us well can really help. Parents are not to be ignored, though they may have ambitions that we do not share. Even a parent's violent tirade against a marriage they do not like for some irrelevant

87

reason is likely to contain some home truths and some apposite judgments which will help us. If the marriage is right we can cheerfully face all the adverse criticisms. If it is doubtful we want to hear both sides of the argument.

Marriage will solve some of the problems. It is the divinely ordained goal of sex and we are right to hope that it will meet some of the deep needs of our humanity. But it will create other problems and these problems need to be faced or we shall only exchange one set for a far worse set. It may not even solve our problem of sex, as the all-too-frequent triangle bears witness. We should therefore enter it only when we have tried to face what it means and to ensure that we ourselves are ready for and worthy of it and that in every way it has God's approval. Then we can approach it with thankful joy and whole-hearted enthusiasm.

9 St Paul on marriage

IN EPHESIANS 5 and the early part of 1 Timothy 4, and in a number of other passages, the apostle Paul sets out an exalted and positive view of marriage which is quite unmistakable. It is therefore the more surprising when we turn to 1 Corinthians 7 to find him apparently advocating marriage simply as an alternative to sin and adopting what appears to be such a grudging and negative view of it as to remind us of a crusty old bachelor.

But it needs to be asked whether in fact that is Paul's attitude in this passage. A closer study of the chapter shows, first, that Paul was not setting out systematic teaching on marriage, but only answering certain limited questions, and second, that his attitude is in fact a warm-hearted approval of marriage, qualified only by certain very practical considerations. He emphasizes that there is real danger of misusing God's gifts. He does not play down marriage but warns of some of the dangers of both marriage and celibacy.

The background is also important. First, Corinth was a notoriously wicked city and it is evident that even the church had been to some extent infected by the prevailing standards (see 1 Corinthians 5 and 6). Immorality seems to have been a very real danger for anyone remaining unmarried, because of the prevailing influences. Second, the apostle appears to have been asked not so much about marriage, as about celibacy and whether it was not a Christian ideal to be free from marriage ties even, possibly, to the extent of leaving your married partner. The questions are not preserved for us, but the argument of the passage can be stated in a very free paraphrase-with-comment as follows:

'Now as to the question about which you wrote: it is good, though not always better, to be unmarried (*i.e.*, it is not only allowable but healthy and good). Nevertheless, God has ordained marriage and it is normally best for everyone to have his own (one) wife or husband. The only alternative to this as the general rule of society is chaotic and shifting relationships, and if people artificially and permanently deny themselves marriage when they are very much in love, there will be chaos. We must pay respect to our human nature and the perfectly right instincts with which God has endowed us. Therefore, married couples must not try to live together as if they were not married, or they will be going against God's endowment and will court disaster. Equally the unmarried must try to find out which gift God has given them; to be married is His gift to some and to be unmarried is His gift to others (verse 7). Both, therefore, should be received with thankfulness as His all-wise provision. Don't try to be what God did not intend. Nevertheless, there are good practical reasons (to be mentioned later) why I, Paul, could wish that people had the gift that God has given me – that of being contentedly and happily single. Let us apply them to different cases.'

1. *Unmarried men and widows* (verses 8, 9). 'It is perfectly all right for them to continue unmarried, as I, Paul, have done. But if their gift does not lie this way, and it puts them under constant and acute strain and temptation, let them marry, not as a second best but because God has so gifted them. It is certainly better to marry than to be consumed with lawful desires or, of course, unlawful ones. For instance, there are people who, while very much in love or at least deeply attracted to someone, might feel that it was not "spiritual" to marry, or even that it was sinful to do so. This is quite a wrong view. Celibacy is not more virtuous than the married state (or vice versa) and if circumstances and temperament place you so that you "burn" with a pure desire for a lifelong partnership with another Christian, then it is best to marry. Nevertheless, do not take marriage for granted. There are many advantages in being single.'

2. *The married* (verses 10–24). 'There is a specific commandment of our Lord Himself. The Christian must not leave his or her partner and, if they have separated, they are not free to marry someone else. The Lord's own teaching, however, does not mention the case of a Christian married to a non-Christian. Here again the Christian should never initiate a separation, but if the unbeliever deserts you then it cannot be helped. In such a case you are not under bondage to reclaim your partner at all costs. Let him or her go but the ideal is to live together in peace.' (Some people see

in verse 15 'not bound' a ground not only of separation but also of divorce and freedom to re-marry. This seems unlikely in view of verses 11 and 39 and the fact that such a ground of divorce is not even hinted at anywhere in the Bible.)

'This raises a general principle (verses 17–24). We must believe in God's providential overruling of our circumstances even before we were converted and, therefore, the general rule is to continue in that state of life in which you found yourself when you became a Christian. This applies to circumcision and uncircumcision, to slavery and freedom (though it is proper to take an opportunity of getting your freedom if it comes), and also to being married or single.'

3. *Unmarried women and young people generally* (verses 25–38). (Paul tackles this from the standpoint of the responsible parent, who, in those days, had to make the decision for his daughter. With no great adaptation we may apply it to unmarried men and women today.)

'Here again Christ has left no commandment and, indeed, since there is no right and wrong about it in an absolute sense I, Paul, can only give you my advice as that of an experienced and consistent apostle. I will not lay down a rule, because no rule is possible, but the following factors ought to be borne in mind.

'We are (in AD 55) in a period of distress and impending persecution. Every persecutor knows that a man or woman who cannot be got at directly can often be got at through his family. Therefore, married people are in for a time of acute anxieties and troubles (as, indeed, in some countries today for those in certain types of missionary work and other walks of life). I would spare you these and, therefore, advise against marriage, though please note that I do not say that marriage is sin. I only say that it is asking for trouble at this present time and I would spare you trouble.

'The opportunity for Christian work and witness is in any case short and limited. We must live as loose to the world, our possessions and our families as we possibly can. All these things are merely temporary and there is work of eternal value to do.

'There is also real danger of selfishness (verses 29–34). Married couples (or courting couples) easily become far too wrapped up in one another and their mutual concern. We all know couples who are a dead loss to their fellow-Christians, to the church and to everyone else, and who seem to become increasingly selfish and small-minded. It need not be so and we must fight against it. There are eternal issues at stake. We must see marriage and all that leads up to it in its proper proportions. But married people cannot shirk their home responsibilities and these are much more limiting than the unmarried often realize. If you are married you have important duties at home which you must discharge and you cannot concentrate without distraction on the Lord's service.

'These are powerful reasons for avoiding marriage at least while you are young (verse 36). Do consider the great privilege of Christian service which is open in special degree for the unmarried. If you would only postpone marriage until you feel that it will be rather late if you leave it any longer (verse 36) there are tremendous spheres of service open to you, and for some there will be the high calling of a permanently unmarried life.

'Now please realize that I do not say this at all in order to curtail your liberty (verse 35) but only to help you towards the best and, if circumstances or temperament lead you in another direction, there is nothing wrong in getting married. It is a good gift of God (verse 36). But the man or woman who sets himself to be unmarried for the sake of Christian service and who can do so without wavering will be even more highly privileged. Marriage is a good thing but, if celibacy is equally possible for you, then (and then only) celibacy is better (verses 37, 38).'

All this may be applied to ourselves in various ways.

1. We should not criticize others for what they do, nor should we necessarily follow the examples of our Christian leaders. Each has his own gift in the matter. This gift is not only a matter of temperament, but is also one of circumstances, including whether you have ever met a suitable partner and really cared for him or her at all deeply. It covers many aspects of personal circumstance which vary enormously from one to another. Those who slavishly follow the man or woman through whom they were converted, for instance, are not at this point following scriptural principle and they are asking for trouble.

2. We should recognize that within fairly wide limits this is not a matter of marriage being right or wrong, but of its being expedient or inexpedient, wise or unwise.

3. We should not regard marriage as a matter of course and certainly not when we are young. It will probably be best to put it out of our mind for the present while we are students, and to seek to be completely

free for the Lord's service now. To be constantly wife- or husband-hunting while still a student is exceedingly unwise.

4. We should respect the vocation of others and not seek to disturb their feelings and purposes unless we are really serious. Light-heartedly to stir up the affections of another may make it permanently more difficult for him to settle to a vocation of a single teacher or missionary, for instance. It is wrong on other grounds, too; but it can also seriously hinder Christian work and cause grave personal hurt to those whose vocation turns out to be in the single state.

5. If in God's plan we are paired or married we must take particular care not to be selfish about it. We have to think how we may better serve God because of this calling, not how we may opt out. The plea 'I have married a wife, and therefore I cannot come' (or 'I have got a girl/boy friend') has a very ominous ring about it.

6. In God's economy there is no 'shelf', but only a variety of callings. We must not panic into experimental and superficial friendships because He has not yet seen fit to introduce us to our future life partner. He knows best.

7. Finally, the challenge which Paul presents to us in this passage is one which we should respect and never resent if we are spiritually minded. The Christian who wilts or grumbles against a practical challenge of this sort is clearly not one whose delight is in pleasing God at all costs.